THE WIT
AND
WISDOM OF
Jane Austen

Edited by Joelle Herr

Kennebunkport, ME

CONTENTS

INTRODUCTION

*"Where an opinion is general,
it is usually correct."*

—Mary Crawford, *Mansfield Park*

$\mathscr{V}$irginia Woolf declared Jane Austen "the most perfect artist among women, the writer whose books are immortal." Eudora Welty believed that "Jane Austen's work at its best seems as nearly flawless as any fiction could be."

J. K. Rowling has referred to Jane as "the pinnacle to which all other authors aspire." And thousands of self-professed "Janeites" enthusiastically celebrate the author, reading and rereading and discussing her works.

And so the "general" (and, therefore, "correct") opinion appears to be resounding: the world loves Jane Austen.

Her oeuvre is small—most notably six completed novels, two partial novels, three volumes of juvenilia—and none of the four novels published during her lifetime were attributed to her. The little of what we know about Jane's life has been pieced together from her letters (only about 160 exist, out of an estimated 3,000 that she wrote), but it seems unlikely that she could have fathomed just how popular and beloved her works would become. *Pride and Prejudice*, alone, has sold an astounding twenty million copies since it was first published in 1813.

Born on December 16, 1775, in the small English village of Steventon, Jane was the seventh of eight children.

Though her father—a rector—and mother both descended from respected gentry, they were by no means wealthy. Aside from a brief stint at boarding school, Jane received no formal education. She was, however, an avid reader, devouring the books in her father's extensive library. Her family encouraged her writing pursuits, especially her father, who gave her a series of journals, which she filled with stories, verse, and a thirty-four-page parody called "The History of England," illustrated by her sister, Cassandra.

By the age of twenty-five, Austen had completed manuscripts of *Sense and Sensibility*, *Pride and Prejudice*, and *Northanger Abbey*. She then experienced a nearly ten-year-long dry spell, during which her father and brother Henry made a couple of unsuccessful attempts to get her works published. Henry eventually found a publisher for *Sense and Sensibility*, which was released in 1811. *Pride and Prejudice* hit the shelves in 1813, followed by *Mansfield Park* in 1814, and *Emma* in 1815. *Persuasion* and *Northanger Abbey* were published together in 1817, six months after Jane's untimely death at the age of forty-one.

Though all of Jane's novels are very much of a specific time (late 1700s, early 1800s) and place (mostly rural England), her characters are iconic and relatable on many levels, her wit and wisdom perfectly timeless. Her "universal truths" touch upon a broad range of topics, from friendship ("the finest balm for the pangs of disappointed love") to human nature ("needs more lessons than a weekly sermon can convey") to happiness ("you must be the best judge of your own").

On the following pages, you'll find a veritable treasure trove of 175 quotes—quips and words of wisdom, divided into ten topics—from Austen's novels and private letters. Complementing Jane's words are more than fifty delightful 1890s illustrations—depicting such classic scenes as Darcy professing his love to Elizabeth, Willoughby whisking an injured Marianne through the rain, and Captain Wentworth silently sliding his letter across the desk to Anne—by artists H. M. and C. E. Brock, who were brothers, and Hugh Thomson. Finally, twenty tidbits about Jane's life will provide some context to the quotes and raise your Austen IQ to true Janeite level.

Get ready to smile, chuckle, nod, sigh, and swoon. Much like Captain Benwick—who "will sit poring over his book, and not know when a person speaks to him, or when one drops one's scissors, or anything that happens"—you may become completely absorbed as you peruse the wit and wisdom of one of the greatest and most beloved writers of all time.

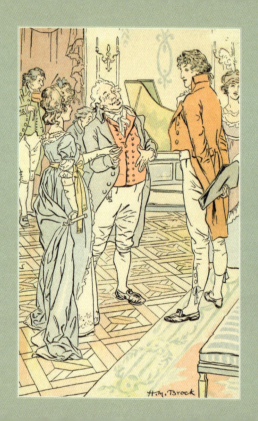

SPORT
FOR OUR
NEIGHBORS:

ON SOCIETY

*Every neighborhood
should have a great lady.*

—Sanditon

*If adventures will not befall a
young lady in her own village,
she must seek them abroad.*

—Northanger Abbey

It is a truth universally acknowledged,
that a single man in possession
of a good fortune must be in want
of a wife. However little known
the feelings or views of such
a man may be on his first entering
a neighborhood, this truth is so well
fixed in the minds of the surrounding
families, that he is considered
the rightful property of some one
or other of their daughters.

—*Pride and Prejudice*

A Royal Request

In 1815, as she was preparing *Emma* for publication, Jane was informed that the prince regent—who had taken over for his father, "mad" King George III, in 1811— was a fan of her novels. Court librarian James Stanier Clarke let Austen know that she would be "at liberty" to dedicate her next work to the prince. In reality, though, the admiration was not mutual. In private letters, Jane had criticized the prince, who was known for his extravagant spending and womanizing ways. Despite this, Jane was well aware that the suggestion was really more of an order, and so the dedication was made. The text— likely written by her publisher—referred to Jane as the prince regent's "dutiful and obedient humble servant."

"*A single woman*, with a very narrow income, must be a ridiculous, disagreeable old maid—the proper sport of boys and girls—but a single woman, of good fortune, is always respectable, and may be as sensible and pleasant as any body else."

—Emma Woodhouse, *Emma*

"In a country neighborhood you move in a very confined and unvarying society."

—Mr. Darcy, *Pride and Prejudice*

"*Give a girl an education, and introduce her properly into the world, and ten to one but she has the means of settling well, without further expense to anybody.*"

—Mrs. Norris, *Mansfield Park*

"We are to have a tiny party here tonight; I hate tiny parties—they force one into constant exertion."

—letter to Cassandra Austen, May 21–22, 1801

"I speak what appears to me the general opinion; and where an opinion is general, it is usually correct."

—Mary Crawford, *Mansfield Park*

"There are few people whom I really love, and still fewer of whom I think well. The more I see of the world, the more am I dissatisfied with it; and every day confirms my belief of the inconsistency of all human characters, and of the little dependence that can be placed on the appearance of merit or sense."

—Elizabeth Bennet, *Pride and Prejudice*

*"Where shall I begin?
Which of all my important
nothings shall I tell you first?"*

—letter to Cassandra Austen, June 15–17, 1808

*"A very narrow income has a
tendency to contract the mind,
and sour the temper."*

—Emma Woodhouse, *Emma*

A LOVE OF DANCE

"Jane was fond of dancing, and excelled in it," according to her brother Henry. Many of Jane's letters to her sister, Cassandra, are filled with playful gossip and details of various dinner parties, balls, and other gatherings where socializing and dancing—and sometimes husband-seeking—went hand in hand. In one such letter (dated December 24–26, 1798), Jane boasted: "There were twenty dances, and I danced them all, and without fatigue. I was glad to find myself capable of dancing so much and with so much satisfaction as I did."

"*For what do we live,
but to make sport
for our neighbors,
and laugh at them
in our turn?*"

—Mr. Bennet, *Pride and Prejudice*

"Every savage can dance."

—Mr. Darcy, *Pride and Prejudice*

There certainly are not so many
men of large fortune in
the world as there are pretty
women to deserve them.

—*Mansfield Park*

"*I cannot* imagine how a man can have the impudence to come into a family party for three days, where he is quite a stranger, unless he knows himself to be agreeable on undoubted authority."

—letter to Cassandra Austen, October 14–15, 1813

"He is a gentleman;
I am a gentleman's
daughter; so far
we are equal."

—Elizabeth Bennet, *Pride and Prejudice*

CLEVER, WELL~INFORMED PEOPLE:

"There is nothing I would not do for those who are really my friends. I have no notion of loving people by halves; it is not my nature. My attachments are always excessively strong."

—Isabella Thorpe, *Northanger Abbey*

A Best Friend

No one was closer to Jane than her beloved sister, Cassandra. Just under three years apart in age, neither ever married, but both were devoted to tending to the needs of their brothers' large families. When this caused them to be apart, Jane and Cassandra exchanged lengthy letters full of love, humor, and gossip. When they were together, they shared a bedroom, in which they chatted and read aloud to each other. Upon Jane's death, Cassandra wrote, "I have lost a treasure, such a sister, such a friend as never can have been surpassed."

"*Luckily the pleasures of friendship, of unreserved conversation, of similarity of taste and opinions, will make good amends for orange wine.*"

—letter to Cassandra Austen, June 30–July 1, 1808

She had been a friend and companion such as few possessed: intelligent, well-informed, useful, gentle, knowing all the ways of the family, interested in all its concerns, and peculiarly interested in herself, in every pleasure, every scheme of hers—one to whom she could speak every thought as it arose, and who had such an affection for her as could never find fault.

—*Emma*

"*You have good sense, and a sweet temper, and I am sure you have a grateful heart that could never receive kindness without wishing to return it. I do not know any better qualifications for a friend and companion.*"

—Edmund Bertram, *Mansfield Park*

Friendship is certainly
the finest balm for the
pangs of disappointed love.

—*Northanger Abbey*

"Mr. Wickham is blessed with such
happy manners as may ensure
his *making* friends—whether he
may be equally capable of
retaining them, is less certain."

—Mr. Darcy, *Pride and Prejudice*

"Business, you know,
may bring money,
but friendship
hardly ever does."

—Mr. Knightley, *Emma*

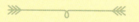

A DEVOTED COUSIN

Aside from her beloved sister, Jane's dearest friend and confidant was her cousin, Eliza. Born in India, Eliza—fourteen years Jane's senior—was beautiful and exotic, perhaps the product of an affair between her mother and prominent statesman Warren Hastings. After her French-aristocrat husband was executed during the French Revolution, Eliza returned to England, charming her Austen cousins with her wit and vivaciousness. She eventually married Jane's brother Henry. Despite their age difference, Jane and Eliza became close, forging a friendship that would last nearly twenty years until Eliza's death in 1813.

"There is nothing so bad as parting with one's friends. One seems so forlorn without them."

—Mrs. Bennet, *Pride and Prejudice*

"*My idea of good company, Mr. Elliot, is the company of clever, well-informed people, who have a great deal of conversation; that is what I call good company.*"

—Anne Elliot, *Persuasion*

"*Give me* but a little cheerful company, let me only have the company of the people I love, let me only be where I like and with whom I like, and the devil take the rest, say I."

—John Thorpe, *Northanger Abbey*

C.E. Brock 1898

NONE
BUT YOU:

ON LOVE

To be fond of dancing was a certain step towards falling in love.

—*Pride and Prejudice*

"In vain I have struggled. It will not do. My feelings will not be repressed. You must allow me to tell you how ardently I admire and love you."

—Mr. Darcy, *Pride and Prejudice*

First Love

In late 1795, Jane met Tom Lefroy (1776–1869), whom she described in a letter (dated January 9–10, 1796) to her sister as a "very gentlemanlike, good-looking, pleasant young man." Lefroy was Irish, visiting family in Hampshire during a break from studying to become a barrister. According to Jane's letters, they danced at three balls together, and it appears that they were quite fond of each other. However, a match was not to be. Tom halted the flirtation and returned to Ireland, likely feeling pressure from his family to marry a woman of at least some fortune. Years later, Tom's nephew confirmed that his uncle had admitted to loving Jane, though he qualified it as "a boyish love."

A young woman, pretty, lively,
with a harp as elegant
as herself, and both placed near
a window, cut down to
the ground, and opening on
a little lawn, surrounded
by shrubs in the rich foliage
of summer, was enough
to catch any man's heart.

—Mansfield Park

"*I cannot* fix on the hour,
or the spot, or the look,
or the words,
which laid the foundation.
It is too long ago.
I was in the middle before
I knew that I *had* begun."

—Mr. Darcy, *Pride and Prejudice*

"This sensation of listlessness,
weariness, stupidity,
this disinclination to sit down
and employ myself, this feeling
of every thing's being dull
and insipid about the house!
I must be in love; I should
be the oddest creature
in the world if I were not."

—Emma Woodhouse, *Emma*

"Next to being married,
a girl likes to be crossed a little
in love now and then."

—Mr. Bennet, *Pride and Prejudice*

"I suppose there may be
a hundred different
ways of being in love."

—Emma Woodhouse, *Emma*

He was in love, very much in love; and it was a love which, operating on an active, sanguine spirit, of more warmth than delicacy, made her affection appear of greater consequence because it was withheld, and determined him to have the glory, as well as the felicity, of forcing her to love him.

—*Mansfield Park*

"Where the heart is really attached, I know very well how little one can be pleased with the attention of anybody else."

—Isabella Thorpe, *Northanger Abbey*

"I must speak to you by such means as are within my reach. You pierce my soul. I am half agony, half hope. Tell me not that I am too late, that such precious feelings are gone for ever. I offer myself to you again with a heart even more your own than when you almost broke it, eight years and a half ago. Dare not say that man forgets sooner than woman, that his love has an earlier death. I have loved none but you."

—Captain Wentworth, *Persuasion*

A Topic of Discussion

Over the last two centuries, Jane's love life—or lack thereof—has been much examined and dissected. It's the subject of countless articles and books, most notably *Dear Jane* by Constance Pilgrim (1971) and *Becoming Jane Austen* by Jon Spence (2003). Rudyard Kipling (1865–1936) even entered the fray with his 1924 poem "Jane's Marriage." In it, upon arriving in heaven, Jane is granted one wish—love—and is reunited with a sailor she is rumored to have fallen in love with before his untimely death at sea.

If it be true, as a celebrated writer
has maintained, that no young lady
can be justified in falling
in love before the gentleman's love
is declared, it must be very improper
that a young lady should dream
of a gentleman before the gentleman
is first known to have dreamt of her.

—*Northanger Abbey*

There could have been no two hearts so open,
no tastes so similar, no feelings so
in unison, no countenances so beloved.

—*Persuasion*

"*Beware how you
give your heart.*"

—James Morland, *Northanger Abbey*

"*The more I know of the world, the more am I convinced that I shall never see a man whom I can really love. I require so much!*"

—Marianne Dashwood, *Sense and Sensibility*

Elizabeth, feeling all the more than common
awkwardness and anxiety of his situation,
now forced herself to speak; and immediately,
though not very fluently, gave him to
understand that her sentiments had undergone
so material a change since the period to which
he alluded, as to make her receive with gratitude
and pleasure his present assurances.
The happiness which this reply produced was
such as he had probably never felt before,
and he expressed himself on the occasion
as sensibly and as warmly as a man
violently in love can be supposed to be.

—*Pride and Prejudice*

"There is no charm equal to tenderness of heart."

—Emma Woodhouse, *Emma*

Prettier musings of high-wrought love and eternal constancy could never have passed along the streets of Bath than Anne was sporting with from Camden-place to Westgate-buildings. It was almost enough to spread purification and perfume all the way.

—*Persuasion*

*"If I loved you less,
I might be able
to talk about it more."*

—Mr. Knightley, *Emma*

C. E. Brock 1898

An
Excellent
Match:

"It is not every
man's fate to marry
the woman
who loves him best."

—Emma Woodhouse, *Emma*

"*My dear* Alicia, of what a mistake were you guilty in marrying a man of his age! Just old enough to be formal, ungovernable, and to have the gout; too old to be agreeable, too young to die."

—Lady Susan Vernon, *Lady Susan*

"You mistake me, my dear. I have a high respect for your nerves. They are my old friends. I have heard you mention them with consideration these last twenty years at least."

—Mr. Bennet, *Pride and Prejudice*

She had only two daughters, both of whom she had lived to see respectably married, and she had now therefore nothing to do but to marry all the rest of the world.

—*Sense and Sensibility*

A Proposal

On December 2, 1802, Jane received her only known marriage proposal. She was nearly twenty-seven, and her suitor was Harris Bigg-Wither, who was five years her junior, heir to a number of grand estates, and neither dashing nor handsome. It was likely not a romantic gesture, but one of practicality, as Jane was friends with Harris' sisters, and he was in want of a wife. Jane said yes but, after sleeping on it, retracted her acceptance the next day. In the end, she had decided that she could not marry without love.

It would be an excellent match,
for he was rich,
and she was handsome.

—*Sense and Sensibility*

"Happiness in marriage is
entirely a matter of chance."

—Charlotte Lucas, *Pride and Prejudice*

"Mrs. John Lyford is so much pleased with the state of widowhood as to be going to put in for being a widow again; she is to marry a Mr. Fendall, a banker in Gloucester, a man of very good fortune, but considerably older than herself and with three little children."

—letter to Cassandra Austen, January 8–9, 1801

It was a union that must have been to the advantage of both; by her ease and liveliness, his mind might have been softened, his manners improved; and from his judgment, information, and knowledge of the world, she must have received benefit of greater importance.

—*Pride and Prejudice*

MATRIMONIAL ADVICE

More than a decade after turning down her one marriage proposal, Jane counseled her niece Fanny (1793–1882) during her own to-marry-or-not-to-marry conundrum. After Fanny found her feelings cooling toward a young man she had at one point felt quite strongly about, she turned to her aunt for advice. A bit wishy-washy in her response, Jane ultimately advised against the match. In a letter (dated November 18–20, 1814), Jane told the twenty-one-year-old, "Anything is to be preferred or endured rather than marrying without affection." For years, it seemed that Fanny might follow her aunts down the path to spinsterhood, but she did eventually marry at the age of twenty-seven.

Had Elizabeth's opinion been all drawn from her own family, she could not have formed a very pleasing picture of conjugal felicity or domestic comfort. Her father, captivated by youth and beauty, and that appearance of good-humor which youth and beauty generally give, had married a woman whose weak understanding and illiberal mind had very early in their marriage put an end to all real affection for her. Respect, esteem, and confidence had vanished for ever; and all his views of domestic happiness were overthrown.

—*Pride and Prejudice*

"As long as we could be together, nothing ever ailed me, and I never met with the smallest inconvenience."

—Mrs. Croft, *Persuasion*

"*I pay* very little regard . . .
to what any young person says
on the subject of marriage.
If they profess a disinclination
for it, I only set it down
that they have not yet seen
the right person."

—Mrs. Grant, *Mansfield Park*

"If a woman *doubts* as to whether she should accept a man or not, she certainly ought to refuse him. If she can hesitate as to 'Yes,' she ought to say 'No' directly. It is not a state to be safely entered into with doubtful feelings, with half a heart."

—Emma Woodhouse, *Emma*

It was a very proper wedding.
The bride was elegantly dressed;
the two bridesmaids were duly
inferior; her father gave her away;
her mother stood with salts
in her hand, expecting
to be agitated; her aunt tried
to cry; and the service was
impressively read by Dr. Grant.

—*Mansfield Park*

"Oh! What a loss it will be when you are married. You are too agreeable in your single state, too agreeable as a niece. I shall hate when your delicious play of mind is all settled down into conjugal and maternal affections."

—letter to Fanny Knight, February 20–21, 1817

"People that marry can never part, but must go and keep house together. People that dance only stand opposite each other in a long room for half an hour."

—Catherine Morland, *Northanger Abbey*

Marianne could never love by halves; and her whole heart became, in time, as much devoted to her husband, as it had once been to Willoughby.

—*Sense and Sensibility*

C.E. Brock. 1898.

JUDGE FROM

FROM

PROBABILITIES:

ON WOMEN VS. MEN

"*That* would be
the greatest misfortune
of all! To find a man
agreeable whom one
is determined to hate!
Do not wish
me such an evil."

—Elizabeth Bennet, *Pride and Prejudice*

"A man does not recover from such a devotion of the heart to such a woman! He ought not—he does not."

—Captain Wentworth, *Persuasion*

"I shall not pay them any such compliment, I assure you. I have no notion of treating men with such respect. That is the way to spoil them."

—Isabella Thorpe, *Northanger Abbey*

"I could easily forgive *his* pride, if he had not mortified *mine*."

—Elizabeth Bennet, *Pride and Prejudice*

A FAVORITE HEROINE

Like most writers, Jane was highly invested in her works, referring to her first copy of *Pride and Prejudice* as "my own darling child." She was especially fond of that novel's heroine, Elizabeth Bennet. In a letter to Cassandra (dated January 29, 1813), Jane wrote of Lizzie, "I must confess that I think her as delightful a creature as ever appeared in print, and how I shall be able to tolerate those who do not like her at least, I do not know." She also had a fondness for *Persuasion*'s Anne Elliot, telling her niece Fanny (in a letter dated March 23–25, 1817), "You may like the heroine, as she is almost too good for me."

"*We certainly* do not forget you as soon as you forget us. It is, perhaps, our fate rather than our merit. We cannot help ourselves. We live at home, quiet, confined, and our feelings prey upon us. You are forced on exertion. You have always a profession, pursuits, business of some sort or other, to take you back into the world immediately, and continual occupation and change soon weaken impressions."

—Anne Elliot, *Persuasion*

"No, no, it is not man's nature. I will not allow it to be more man's nature than woman's to be inconstant and forget those they do love, or have loved. I believe the reverse. I believe in a true analogy between our bodily frames and our mental; and that as our bodies are the strongest, so are our feelings; capable of bearing most rough usage, and riding out the heaviest weather."

—Captain Harville, *Persuasion*

"*All the privilege I claim for my own sex (it is not a very enviable one; you need not covet it), is that of loving longest, when existence or when hope is gone.*"

—Anne Elliot, *Persuasion*

"*The world must judge from probabilities; she had nothing against her but her husband, and her conscience.*"

—Lady Susan Vernon, *Lady Susan*

"I hate to hear you talking so, like a fine gentleman, and as if women were all fine ladies, instead of rational creatures. We none of us expect to be in smooth water all our days."

—Mrs. Croft, *Persuasion*

Where people wish to attach,
they should always be ignorant.
To come with a well-informed mind is to
come with an inability of administering
to the vanity of others, which a sensible
person would always wish to avoid.
A woman especially, if she have
the misfortune of knowing anything,
should conceal it as well as she can.

—*Northanger Abbey*

"By a Lady"

Even though Jane's contemporaries included many successful women publishing under their own names—including Frances (Fanny) Burney, Maria Edgeworth, and Ann Radcliffe—they often encountered condescension in the press and among readers just for being women. And so many women writers opted to publish anonymously or under male pseudonyms. Jane chose the former option. In 1811, her first book, *Sense and Sensibility*, was published as "By a Lady." In 1813, the title page of *Pride and Prejudice* featured "By the Author of 'Sense and Sensibility.'" Though her identity was known among certain literary circles, she wasn't officially outed as the author of her works until after her death.

"A lady's imagination is very rapid; it jumps from admiration to love, from love to matrimony, in a moment."

—Mr. Darcy, *Pride and Prejudice*

"Do not consider me now as an elegant female, intending to plague you, but as a rational creature, speaking the truth from her heart."

—Elizabeth Bennet, *Pride and Prejudice*

C.E.Brock
1895

"Why did you dance four dances with so stupid a man? Why not rather dance two of them with some elegant brother-officer who was struck with your appearance as soon as you entered the room?"

—letter to Cassandra Austen, January 14–16, 1801

"One half of the world cannot understand the pleasures of the other."

—Emma Woodhouse, *Emma*

"If there is any thing disagreeable going on, men are always sure to get out of it."

—Mary Musgrove, *Persuasion*

"It is always incomprehensible to a man that a woman should ever refuse an offer of marriage. A man always imagines a woman to be ready for any body who asks her."

—Emma Woodhouse, *Emma*

"*Miss Morland, no one can think more highly of the understanding of women than I do. In my opinion, nature has given them so much that they never find it necessary to use more than half.*"

—Henry Tilney, *Northanger Abbey*

"If I could but know his heart, everything would become easy."

—Marianne Dashwood, *Sense and Sensibility*

"I write only to bid you farewell, the spell is removed; I see you as you are."

—Reginald De Courcy, *Lady Susan*

"Men of sense,
whatever you choose
to say, do not
want silly wives."

—Mr. Knightley, *Emma*

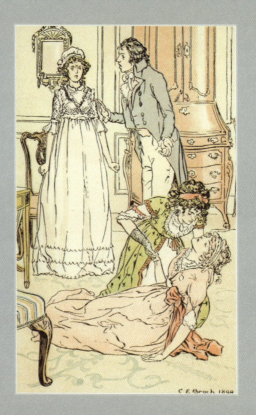

C E Brock 1898

No Hope
of a
Cure:

ON HUMAN NATURE

"*I will be calm. I will be mistress of myself.*"

—Elinor Dashwood, *Sense and Sensibility*

"*We have all a better guide in ourselves, if we would attend to it, than any other person can be.*"

—Fanny Price, *Mansfield Park*

"I cannot forget the follies and vices of others so soon as I ought, nor their offenses against myself. My feelings are not puffed about with every attempt to move them. My temper would perhaps be called resentful. My good opinion once lost, is lost forever."

—Mr. Darcy, *Pride and Prejudice*

"What one means one day, you know, one may not mean the next. Circumstances change, opinions alter."

—Isabella Thorpe, *Northanger Abbey*

*"It is particularly
incumbent on those
who never change
their opinion,
to be secure of judging
properly at first."*

—Elizabeth Bennet, *Pride and Prejudice*

ORIGINAL TITLES

As happens with many books, the titles of most of Jane's novels changed at some point between writing and publication. *Sense and Sensibility* was originally titled "Elinor and Marianne." *Pride and Prejudice* was called "First Impressions." *Northanger Abbey* went by "Susan." And she referred to *Persuasion*—which was published posthumously—as "The Elliots."

Seldom, very seldom,
does complete truth belong
to any human disclosure;
seldom can it happen
that something is
not a little disguised,
or a little mistaken.

—*Emma*

Nobody minds
having what is too
good for them.

—*Mansfield Park*

"I do not know whether it ought to be so, but certainly silly things do cease to be silly if they are done by sensible people in an impudent way. Wickedness is always wickedness, but folly is not always folly."

—Emma Woodhouse, *Emma*

"*Nothing is* more deceitful than the appearance of humility. It is often only carelessness of opinion, and sometimes an indirect boast."

—Mr. Darcy, *Pride and Prejudice*

"Selfishness must always be forgiven, you know, because there is no hope of a cure."

—Mary Crawford, *Mansfield Park*

"There is a stubbornness about me that never can bear to be frightened at the will of others. My courage always rises at every attempt to intimidate me."

—Elizabeth Bennet, *Pride and Prejudice*

"She is a selfish, hypocritical woman, and I have no opinion of her."

—Mrs. Bennet, *Pride and Prejudice*

*"One man's ways may be
as good as another's,
but we all like our own best."*

—Admiral Croft, *Persuasion*

*Human nature needs more lessons
than a weekly sermon can convey.*

—*Mansfield Park*

"*There will be* little rubs
and disappointments everywhere,
and we are all apt to expect too much;
but then, if one scheme of happiness fails,
human nature turns to another;
if the first calculation is wrong,
we make a second better:
we find comfort somewhere—
and those evil-minded observers,
dearest Mary, who make much of a little,
are more taken in and deceived
than the parties themselves."

—Mrs. Grant, *Mansfield Park*

"*Seven years,
I suppose, are enough
to change every pore
of one's skin and every
feeling of one's mind.*"

—letter to Cassandra Austen, April 8–11, 1805

It was not in her nature, however, to increase her vexations by dwelling on them. She was confident of having performed her duty, and to fret over unavoidable evils, or augment them by anxiety, was no part of her disposition.

—*Pride and Prejudice*

GOSSIP GALORE

Given her relatively isolated, rural life, it's not surprising that Jane's letters brim with gossip—like who's marrying (or courting) whom and who wore what to the latest ball. In a letter to Cassandra (dated January 25, 1801), she begged, "I shall expect you to lay in a stock of intelligence that may procure me amusement for a twelvemonth to come." Some gossip veers into not-so-nice territory when referring to women's beauty—or lack thereof. In another missive (dated November 20–21, 1800) to Cassandra, Jane described the attendees of a ball: "There were very few beauties, and, such as there were, were not very handsome."

"Sometimes one is guided by what they say of themselves, and very frequently by what other people say of them, without giving oneself time to deliberate and judge."

—Elinor Dashwood, *Sense and Sensibility*

"*Shyness is* only the effect
of a sense of inferiority in
some way or other. If I could
persuade myself that
my manners were perfectly
easy and graceful,
I should not be shy."

—Edward Ferrars, *Sense and Sensibility*

"Nobody ever feels or acts,
suffers or enjoys as one expects!"

—letter to Cassandra Austen, June 30–July 1, 1808

Wisdom is better than wit, and
in the long run will certainly
have the laugh on her side.

—letter to Fanny Austen, November 18–20, 1814

C E Brock 1898.

A Frivolous Distinction:

ON FASHION, BEAUTY & VANITY

"It is happy for you that you possess the talent of flattering with delicacy. May I ask whether these pleasing attentions proceed from the impulse of the moment, or are the result of previous study?"

—Mr. Bennet, *Pride and Prejudice*

"One man's style
must not
be the rule of
another's."

—Mr. Knightley, *Emma*

Dress is at all times a frivolous distinction, and excessive solicitude about it often destroys its own aim.

—*Northanger Abbey*

"What dreadful hot weather we have! It keeps one in a continual state of inelegance."

—letter to Cassandra Austen, September 18, 1796

"*Such a number of looking-glasses! Oh Lord! There was no getting away from one's self.*"

—Admiral Croft, *Persuasion*

"*Where did you get that quiz of a hat? It makes you look like an old witch.*"

—John Thorpe, *Northanger Abbey*

"*Open carriages are nasty things. A clean gown is not five minutes' wear in them. You are splashed getting in and getting out; and the wind takes your hair and your bonnet in every direction. I hate an open carriage myself.*"

—Mrs. Allen, *Northanger Abbey*

"It is very often nothing but
our own vanity that deceives us.
Women fancy admiration
means more than it does."

—Jane Bennet, *Pride and Prejudice*

"Handsome is as handsome
does; he is therefore
a very ill-looking man."

—letter to Cassandra Austen, January 24, 1813

*It sometimes happens that
a woman is handsomer at
twenty-nine than she was ten
years before; and, generally
speaking, if there has been
neither ill health nor anxiety,
it is a time of life at which
scarcely any charm is lost.*

—*Persuasion*

PORTRAIT OF A LADY

Firsthand written accounts of Jane's appearance vary, though one can deduce from them that she was likely not considered conventionally beautiful. Can you imagine if she had been beautiful on top of being brilliant, generous, witty, charming, and master of the written word? It would have been too much. In any case, Jane is known to have been tall and thin, with hazel eyes and brown hair, which she styled with short curls framing her face, the rest pinned up in the back. She never sat for a formal portrait, but her sister, Cassandra, composed a pencil-and-watercolor sketch of her, which inspired the drawing on page 6.

"But he talked of flannel waistcoats . . . and with me a flannel waistcoat is invariably connected with aches, cramps, rheumatisms, and every species of ailment that can afflict the old and the feeble."

—Marianne Dashwood, *Sense and Sensibility*

"*Vanity* working on a weak head produces every sort of mischief. Nothing so easy as for a young lady to raise her expectations too high."

—Mr. Knightley, *Emma*

To look *almost* pretty
is an acquisition of higher
delight to a girl
who has been looking
plain the first fifteen
years of her life than
a beauty from her
cradle can ever receive.

—*Northanger Abbey*

Vanity was the beginning and the end of Sir Walter Elliot's character; vanity of person and of situation. He had been remarkably handsome in his youth; and, at fifty-four, was still a very fine man. Few women could think more of their personal appearance than he did, nor could the valet of any new made lord be more delighted with the place he held in society. He considered the blessing of beauty as inferior only to the blessing of a baronetcy; and the Sir Walter Elliot who united these gifts was the constant object of his warmest respect and devotion.

—*Persuasion*

*"Had I been in love,
I could not have been
more wretchedly blind!
But vanity, not love,
has been my folly."*

—Elizabeth Bennet, *Pride and Prejudice*

"*Vanity and pride* are different things, though the words are often used synonymously. A person may be proud without being vain. Pride relates more to our opinion of ourselves, vanity to what we would have others think of us."

—Mary Bennet, *Pride and Prejudice*

"My black cap was openly admired by Mrs. Lefroy, and secretly, I imagine, by everybody else in the room."

—letter to Cassandra Austen, December 24–26, 1798

"There goes a strange-looking woman! What an odd gown she has on! How old-fashioned it is!"

—Mrs. Allen, *Northanger Abbey*

CAPS AND GOWNS

Many of Jane's letters to Cassandra feature discussion of fashion—especially hats and dresses, both their own and what others wore. Jane appears to have had an ambivalent view on the topic. At times, she seems to be caught up in it—or to play along. In one letter (dated October 14–15, 1813), she attempted to sell Cassandra on the latest fad: "You must really get some flounces. Are not some of your large stock of white morning gowns just in a happy state for a flounce, too short?" At other times, she seems sick of it all, lamenting in a letter (dated December 24–26, 1798), "I cannot determine what to do about my new gown; I wish such things were to be bought ready-made."

The Miss Bertrams were now fully established
among the belles of the neighborhood;
and as they joined to beauty and brilliant
acquirements a manner naturally easy,
and carefully formed to general civility
and obligingness, they possessed its favor
as well as its admiration. Their vanity
was in such good order that they seemed
to be quite free from it, and gave themselves
no airs; while the praises attending
such behavior, secured and brought round
by their aunt, served to strengthen
them in believing they had no faults.

—*Mansfield Park*

The real evils, indeed, of Emma's situation were the power of having rather too much her own way, and a disposition to think a little too well of herself.

—*Emma*

He had frequently observed, as he walked, that
one handsome face would be followed by thirty,
or five-and-thirty frights; and once,
as he had stood in a shop on Bond Street,
he had counted eighty-seven women go by, one
after another, without there being a tolerable
face among them. It had been a frosty morning,
to be sure, a sharp frost, which hardly one
woman in a thousand could stand the test
of. But still, there certainly were a dreadful
multitude of ugly women in Bath; and
as for the men! They were infinitely worse.
Such scarecrows as the streets were full of!

—*Persuasion*

The world had made him extravagant and vain. Extravagance and vanity had made him cold-hearted and selfish. Vanity, while seeking its own guilty triumph at the expense of another, had involved him in a real attachment, which extravagance, or at least its offspring, necessity, had required to be sacrificed. Each faulty propensity in leading him to evil, had led him likewise to punishment.

—*Sense and Sensibility*

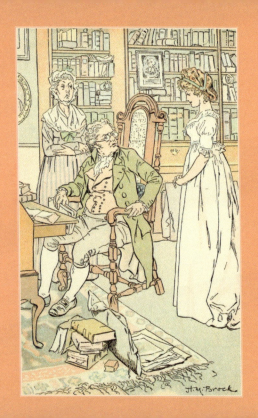

H.M. Brock

THE VULGARITY OF HER NEAREST RELATIONS:

ON FAMILY

"*It is very* unfair to judge of any body's conduct, without an intimate knowledge of their situation. Nobody, who has not been in the interior of a family, can say what the difficulties of any individual of that family may be."

—Emma Woodhouse, *Emma*

"*This is* a most unfortunate affair, and will probably be much talked of. But we must stem the tide of malice, and pour into the wounded bosoms of each other the balm of sisterly consolation."

—Mary Bennet, *Pride and Prejudice*

"What strange creatures brothers are!"

—Mary Crawford, *Mansfield Park*

"An unhappy alternative
is before you, Elizabeth.
From this day you must
be a stranger to one of your
parents. Your mother
will never see you again
if you do *not* marry
Mr. Collins, and I will never
see you again if you *do*."

—Mr. Bennet, *Pride and Prejudice*

A FAMILY'S WIT

In her diary, Jane's niece Fanny recalled, "[Jane] thoroughly enjoyed Crabbe . . . and would sometimes say, in jest, that, if she ever married at all, she could fancy being Mrs. Crabbe." The Crabbe in question was poet George Crabbe (1754–1832), and, indeed, there was a running family joke that Jane wanted to marry him. In a letter to Cassandra (dated September 15, 1813), Jane joked that she was in London and "in agonies—I have not yet seen Mr. Crabbe." After hearing about the death of Mrs. Crabbe the following month, Jane playfully wrote (again, to Cassandra), "I will comfort him as well as I can."

"*But it is* very foolish to ask questions about any young ladies— about any three sisters just grown up; for one knows, without being told, exactly what they are: all very accomplished and pleasing, and one very pretty. There is a beauty in every family; it is a regular thing."

—Mary Crawford, *Mansfield Park*

"We all know him to be a proud, unpleasant sort of man; but this would be nothing if you really liked him."

—Mr. Bennet, *Pride and Prejudice*

"Family squabbling is the greatest evil of all, and we had better do anything than be altogether by the ears."

——Edmund Bertram, *Mansfield Park*

A lady without a family was the very best preserver of furniture in the world.

——*Persuasion*

Another moment and Fanny was in the narrow entrance-passage of the house, and in her mother's arms, who met her there with looks of true kindness, and with features which Fanny loved the more, because they brought her aunt Bertram's before her, and there were her two sisters: Susan, a well-grown fine girl of fourteen, and Betsey, the youngest of the family, about five—both glad to see her in their way, though with no advantage of manner in receiving her. But manner Fanny did not want. Would they but love her, she should be satisfied.

—*Mansfield Park*

A DOTING AUNT

Though—or perhaps *because*—she had no children of her own, Jane relished her role as aunt to her brothers' many children. (Frank and Edward were each father to eleven.) She and her sister, Cassandra, often helped out for months at a time after the birth of a new niece or nephew. Jane was closest to her nieces Fanny, whom she advised on matters of the heart (see page 84), and Anna, whom she advised on matters of the pen (see page 196). In 1869, Jane's nephew James Edward Austen-Leigh published *A Memoir of Jane Austen*, which drew upon her letters and memories of surviving family members who knew her. The book was integral in sparking renewed interest in Jane's works.

"Laugh as much
as you choose, but
you will not laugh me
out of my opinion."

—Jane Bennet, *Pride and Prejudice*

*I believe there is scarcely a young lady
in the United Kingdoms who
would not rather put up with the
misfortune of being sought by a clever,
agreeable man, than have
him driven away by the vulgarity
of her nearest relations.*

—*Mansfield Park*

"I give you joy of our new nephew,
and hope if he ever comes
to be hanged, it will not be till we
are too old to care about it."

—letter to Cassandra Austen, April 25, 1811

A family of ten children will always
be a fine family, where there
are heads and arms and legs
enough for the number.

—*Northanger Abbey*

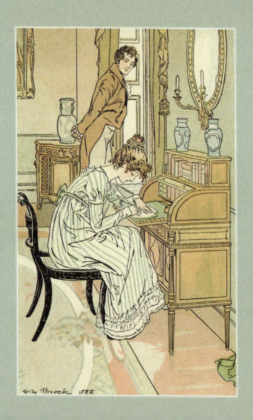

H.M. Brock 1898

PLEASURE IN A
GOOD NOVEL:
ON READING AND WRITING

"The person, be it gentleman or lady, who has not pleasure in a good novel, must be intolerably stupid."

—Henry Tilney, *Northanger Abbey*

With a book he was regardless of time.

—*Pride and Prejudice*

"*Not keep a journal!* How are your absent cousins to understand the tenor of your life in Bath without one? How are the civilities and compliments of every day to be related as they ought to be, unless noted down every evening in a journal? How are your various dresses to be remembered, and the particular style of your complexion, and curl of your hair to be described in all their diversities, without having constant recourse to a journal?"

—Henry Tilney, *Northanger Abbey*

A Mentor

Anna Austen (1793–1872)—daughter of Jane's brother James—was an aspiring writer, herself, and often solicited feedback from her aunt. Austen's editorial suggestions were a brilliant swirl of expert criticism, sincere delight, and, of course, her signature wit. In a letter (dated September 28, 1814) to Anna, Jane offered this sage advice on a particular character: "Devereux Forester's being ruined by his vanity is extremely good; but I wish you would not let him plunge into a 'vortex of dissipation.' I do not object to the thing, but I cannot bear the expression. It is such thorough novel slang— and so old that I dare say Adam met with it in the first novel he opened."

"I do not know what is the matter with me today, but I cannot write quietly; I am always wandering away into some exclamation or other."

—letter to Cassandra Austen, June 11, 1799

"And to all this she must yet add something more substantial, in the improvement of her mind by extensive reading."

—Mr. Darcy, *Price and Prejudice*

"It is a rule with me that a person who can write a long letter with ease cannot write ill."

—Miss Bingley, *Pride and Prejudice*

"He will sit poring over his book, and not know when a person speaks to him, or when one drops one's scissors, or anything that happens."

—Mary Musgrove, *Persuasion*

"Could my ideas flow as fast as the rain in the store-closet, it would be charming."

—letter to Cassandra Austen, January 24, 1809

A Competitor

Sir Walter Scott (1771–1832) was Jane's contemporary and a true literary superstar—a novelist, poet, playwright, and author of many works of historical nonfiction. While Scott praised Austen's works, the admiration was not mutual. In a letter (dated September 28, 1814) to her niece Anna, Jane wrote: "Walter Scott has no business to write novels, especially good ones. It is not fair. He has fame and profit enough as a poet, and should not be taking the bread out of other people's mouths. I do not like him and do not mean to like *Waverley* [Scott's first novel]—but I fear I must." Indeed, *Waverley* (1814) was a smashing hit that was followed by such classics as *Rob Roy* (1817) and *Ivanhoe* (1820).

"Women are the only correspondents to be depended on."

—Mr. Parker, *Sanditon*

"I am quite angry at myself for not writing closer; why is my alphabet so much more sprawly than yours?"

—letter to Cassandra Austen, October 27–28, 1798

"It is very well worthwhile to be tormented for two or three years of one's life, for the sake of being able to read all the rest of it."

—Henry Tilney, *Northanger Abbey*

"I cannot talk of books in a ball-room; my head is always full of something else."

—Elizabeth Bennet, *Pride and Prejudice*

Their taste was strikingly alike. The same books, the same passages were idolized by each—or if any difference appeared, any objection arose, it lasted no longer than till the force of her arguments and the brightness of her eyes could be displayed. He acquiesced in all her decisions, caught all her enthusiasm; and long before his visit concluded, they conversed with the familiarity of a long-established acquaintance.

—*Sense and Sensibility*

He knew her to be clever, to have a quick apprehension as well as good sense, and a fondness for reading, which, properly directed, must be an education in itself.

—*Mansfield Park*

"He and I should not in the least agree, of course, in our ideas of novels and heroines; pictures of perfection, as you know, make me sick and wicked."

—letter to Fanny Knight, March 23–25, 1817

But from fifteen to seventeen
she was in training for a heroine;
she read all such works
as heroines must read to supply
their memories with those
quotations which are so serviceable
and so soothing in the vicissitudes
of their eventful lives.

—*Northanger Abbey*

"Oh! I am delighted with the book! I should like to spend my whole life in reading it."

——Catherine Morland, *Northanger Abbey*

In his library he had been always sure of leisure and tranquility; and though prepared, as he told Elizabeth, to meet with folly and conceit in every other room of the house, he was used to be free from them there.

—*Pride and Prejudice*

"*I declare* after all there is no enjoyment like reading! How much sooner one tires of anything than of a book! When I have a house of my own, I shall be miserable if I have not an excellent library."

—Miss Bingley, *Pride and Prejudice*

The Most Perfect Refreshment:

ON HAPPINESS

"To sit in the shade on a fine day, and look upon verdure, is the most perfect refreshment."

—Fanny Price, *Mansfield Park*

"I wish as well as every body else to be perfectly happy; but, like every body else it must be in my own way."

—Edward Ferrars, *Sense and Sensibility*

"*Know your own happiness. You want nothing but patience—or give it a more fascinating name, call it hope.*"

—Mrs. Dashwood, *Sense and Sensibility*

How little of permanent happiness could belong to a couple who were only brought together because their passions were stronger than their virtue.

—*Pride and Prejudice*

Not So Happy

In 1800, when Jane was twenty-five—with three completed but unpublished novels under her belt—her father decided to retire and hand his position as rector at Steventon over to his oldest son, James. And so Jane, Cassandra, and their parents left the only home Jane had ever known, spending the next decade living a bit of a nomadic life. Austen biographer Claire Tomalin suggests that Jane suffered from depression as a result of this displacement, and that it may be the reason why she put down her pen—her novel-writing pen, at least—for nearly ten years. Thankfully, in 1809, she picked it back up again after settling more permanently in the village of Chawton.

"*He will make you happy, Fanny; I know he will make you happy; but you will make him everything.*"

—Edmund Bertram, *Mansfield Park*

She loved everybody, was interested in everybody's happiness, quick-sighted to everybody's merits; thought herself a most fortunate creature, and surrounded with blessings in such an excellent mother, and so many good neighbors and friends, and a home that wanted for nothing.

—*Emma*

"Give a loose rein
to your fancy, indulge
your imagination
in every possible flight."

—Elizabeth Bennet, *Pride and Prejudice*

Why not seize the pleasure at once?
How often is happiness destroyed
by preparation, foolish preparation!

—Frank Churchill, *Emma*

"I . . . next week shall begin
my operations on my hat,
on which you know my principal
hopes of happiness depend."

—letter to Cassandra Austen, October 27–28, 1798

"*I have been meditating on the very great pleasure which a pair of fine eyes in the face of a pretty woman can bestow.*"

—Mr. Darcy, *Pride and Prejudice*

Every moment had its pleasures and its hopes.

—*Mansfield Park*

"What have wealth or grandeur to do with happiness?"

—Marianne Dashwood, *Sense and Sensibility*

Catherine . . . enjoyed her usual happiness with Henry Tilney, listening with sparkling eyes to everything he said; and, in finding him irresistible, becoming so herself.

—*Northanger Abbey*

"Your countenance perfectly informs me that you were in company last night with the person whom you think the most agreeable in the world, the person who interests you at this present time more than all the rest of the world put together."

—Mrs. Smith, *Persuasion*

"A large income is the best recipe
for happiness I ever heard of."

—Mary Crawford, *Mansfield Park*

"It is so delightful
to have an evening now
and then to oneself."

—Isabella Thorpe, *Northanger Abbey*

"A scheme of which every part promises delight can never be successful."

—Elizabeth Bennet, *Pride and Prejudice*

"I am very glad the new cook
begins so well. Good apple pies
are a considerable part
of our domestic happiness."

—letter to Cassandra Austen, October 17–18, 1815

"You must be the
best judge of your
own happiness."

—Emma Woodhouse, *Emma*

"WITH HIGH GLEE"

In her letters, Jane revealed various causes of momentary happiness to be such simple pleasures as a hat (page 225) and apple pies (page 235). The thing that appeared to give her the most happiness, however, was receiving letters from her dear sister, Cassandra, as evidenced in her ebullient opening lines, such as this one (dated September 23–24, 1813): "Thank you five hundred and forty times for the exquisite piece of workmanship which was brought into the room this morning while we were at breakfast . . . which I read with high glee—much delighted with everything it told, whether good or bad."

Colonel Brandon was now as happy,
as all those who best loved him,
believed he deserved to be.
In Marianne he was consoled for
every past affliction. Her regard and
her society restored his mind
to animation, and his spirits
to cheerfulness; and that Marianne
found her own happiness in forming
his, was equally the persuasion
and delight of each observing friend.

—*Sense and Sensibility*

ART CREDITS

All illustrations from The British Library (https://www.flickr.com/photos/britishlibrary).

p. 6: Jane Austen portrait; p. 12: H. M. Brock illustration from *Pride and Prejudice*; pp. 19 & 22: C. E. Brock illustrations from *Pride and Prejudice*; pp. 26 & 31: Hugh Thomson illustrations from *Sense and Sensibility*; p. 32: H. M. Brock illustration from *Sense and Sensibility*; pp. 35 & 38: Hugh Thomson illustrations from *Mansfield Park*; p. 46: Hugh Thomson illustration from *Persuasion*; p. 48: H. M. Brock illustration from *Sense and Sensibility*; p. 51: C. E. Brock illustration from *Pride and Prejudice*; p. 57: Hugh Thomson illustration from *Northanger Abbey*; p. 60: Hugh Thomson illustration from *Persuasion*; p. 65: C. E. Brock illustration from *Pride and Prejudice*; p. 69: Hugh Thomson illustration from *Sense and Sensibility*; p. 72: C. E. Brock illustration from *Sense and Sensibility*; pp. 76, 82 & 89: C. E. Brock illustrations from

Pride and Prejudice; p. 93: Hugh Thomson illustration from *Emma*; p. 94: C. E. Brock illustration from *Sense and Sensibility*; pp. 98, 106 & 111: C. E. Brock illustrations from *Pride and Prejudice*; p. 114: Hugh Thomson illustration from *Northanger Abbey*; p. 119: Hugh Thomson illustration from *Mansfield Park*; p. 120: C. E. Brock illustration from *Sense and Sensibility*; p. 123: Hugh Thomson illustration from *Mansfield Park*; p. 130: Hugh Thomson illustration from *Sense and Sensibility*; p. 135: C. E. Brock illustration from *Pride and Prejudice*; p. 140: Hugh Thomson illustration from *Sense and Sensibility*; p. 146: C. E. Brock illustration from *Sense and Sensibility*; p. 153: Hugh Thomson illustration from *Mansfield Park*; p. 160: Hugh Thomson illustration from *Northanger Abbey*; p. 164: C. E. Brock illustration from *Pride and Prejudice*; p. 170: Hugh Thomson illustration from *Mansfield Park*; p. 173: Hugh Thomson illustration from *Sense and Sensibility*; p. 174: H. M. Brock illustration from *Pride and Prejudice*; p. 177: Hugh Thomson illustration from *Emma*; p. 182: C. E. Brock illustration from *Pride and Prejudice*; p. 185: Hugh Thomson illustration from *Sense and Sensibility*; p. 189: C. E. Brock illustration from *Pride and Prejudice*; p. 192: H. M. Brock illustration from *Mansfield Park*; pp. 199 & 200: C. E. Brock illustrations from *Pride and Prejudice*; p. 207: Hugh Thomson illustration from *Persuasion*; p. 212: Hugh Thomson illustration from *Northanger Abbey*; p. 214: H. M. Brock illustration from *Pride and Prejudice*; p. 217: Hugh Thomson illustration from *Mansfield Park*; pp. 222, 227 & 231: Hugh Thomson illustrations from *Sense and Sensibility*; p. 234: C. E. Brock illustration from *Pride and Prejudice*

IF YOU HAVE ENJOYED THIS BOOK
OR IT HAS TOUCHED YOUR LIFE IN SOME WAY,
WE WOULD LOVE TO HEAR FROM YOU.

Please send your comments to:
Hallmark Book Feedback
P.O. Box 419034
Mail Drop 100
Kansas City, MO 64141

Or e-mail us at:
booknotes@hallmark.com